The Little Book of Business Wisdom

Brian Banashak

Sixth Printing: May, 2003

Published by Evergreen Press
P.O. Box 191540, Mobile, AL 36619.
(800) 367-8203
info@evergreen777.com

ISBN 1-58169-041-X

To Kathy, Jeff, Jennifer, Joy,
Kerry, Brian, and Rosy.

ACKNOWLEDGEMENTS

Many of the lessons in this book came from close friends and mentors. My thanks to Gary Henley, Charles Simpson, Dow Robinson, Steve Rannells, Don Charest, John Beebee, Rich Raad, and Robert Vande Brake.

I also owe a debt to those writers and speakers whose ideas and concepts have challenged me to grow personally and professionally: Jim Rohn, Jeffrey Lant, Jay Abraham, and Denis Waitley among many others.

Last, but not least, my deepest thanks to my wife Kathy for "hanging in there" with me through 35 plus years of marriage and 14 years of business. She is the best partner a man could have.

TABLE OF CONTENTS

INTRODUCTION

This book began as a poster several years ago. I called it simply "Success Strategy." Over time it grew from seven to fifteen principles for success. At some point it stopped being a poster and grew into an extensive file of notes, reflections, revelations, and theories.

Some of the ideas in this book are quite simple, others you may think profound. Some will be obvious, while others will be new to you. Either way, they are all very *real* to me.

I hope you won't find the title of this book presumptuous. To claim to be wise is folly. Yet these pages reflect the wisdom of the One who designed everything in creation. He is the source and essence of all wisdom, and He is gracious to share that wisdom with those who ask for it and who seek it.

"If any of you lacks wisdom, He should ask God, Who gives generously to all without finding fault, and it will be given to Him" (James 1:5).

I invite you to meander through these pages at your own pace—stopping here and there to reflect.

"Wisdom
is supreme;
therefore
get wisdom.
Though
it cost all you
have, get
understanding"

(Proverbs 4:7 NAS).

Do you have a truth, lesson or saying you want to share? I'd appreciate hearing from you. I'd also like to hear how this book has affected your business.

Address your correspondence c/o Evergreen Press, P.O. Box 91011, Mobile, AL 36691 or e-mail Brian@evergreen777.com.

Find your "one thing" and do it!

"One thing have I desired of the Lord, that will I seek after; that I may dwell in the house of the Lord all the days of my life..."

(Ps. 27:4 emphasis added KJV).

In the popular movie "City Slickers," the old cowboy, Curly, admonishes the younger city-boy-wanna-be-cowboy to find himself by discovering the "one thing." The dude, played by Billy Crystal, asks Curly: "What's the one thing?" Curly replies "That's what *you* gotta figure out."

What is *your* "one thing" that is unique to you? What is your purpose in life? Often it will be the thing you think about most. All other pursuits pale by comparison to finding and fulfilling your destiny.

The business you engage in should be centered around your purpose. Otherwise you'll always be looking over your shoulder, wondering why you don't quite feel at home with your work.

Don't just pursue a career – pursue your purpose.

"To everything there is a season, and a time to every purpose under the heaven"
(Ecclesiastes 3:1 KJV).

As a child, I always wanted to be an inventor. I produced a number of "Rube Goldbergs" growing up. After high school I attended art school, followed by a career in graphic design. Not enough money there, so I started a sales career. As time went on I would become a non-denominational minister, a school principal, an advertising executive, a retail entrepreneur, and a publisher (of course, not all at the same time).

Typically a person will engage in four careers before settling down. Is it because they've finally found their purpose, or have they just gotten tired of starting over? A certain amount of change is good—it rounds you out. But too much change and you start to feel like a tumbleweed.

I've enjoyed the variety in my life. But now, I wish I had found my "one thing" a lot sooner. I'm happy to finally have identified it to guide the rest of my years. I'm looking forward to pursuing my purpose with all of my heart and soul.

Start with realistic, achievable goals.

"Most people plan their vacations with better care than they do their lives."
The Treasury of Quotes by Jim Rohn, ©1994

Your mission statement and business plan will inevitably lead to goal setting. Someone once said: "A goal is a dream with a deadline." Goals—short range and long range—are necessary to fulfill your mission and purpose for being in business.

Someone else has said: "If you can accomplish your dreams in your own strength, they're not big enough." You should think and dream big, but you need to start small. By starting small, your ideas can be proven out and your mistakes won't be as costly. If your goals are too big in the beginning, you may get discouraged and perhaps be tempted to quit. Start with do-able goals to build your confidence.

Goals should be: 1) the means to accomplish your mission; 2) specific and measurable; 3) tied to a deadline or timeline; and 4) worth the time, expense and effort to do them.

How do you spell "success"?

*"Commit to the Lord whatever you do,
and your plans will succeed"*
(Proverbs 16:3).

One definition of *success* says: "the gaining of wealth, position, or the like." Another definition says: "to accomplish what is attempted or intended" (*The American College Dictionary*).

The first definition is usually what comes to mind when we think of success: i.e., stay in business a long time and make a lot of money. For others, who struggle to make their business work, success is spelled "survival."

Now consider the second definition: "to accomplish what is attempted." This is broader. When you set personal or business goals, and reach them, you are by definition, successful. What do *your* goals include: achieving a certain annual sales figure? Treating a certain number of patients?

How about a radically different approach: Set a goal of working less so you can spend more time with your family or do volunteer work. You'd probably make less money; but *how much is enough?*

"But the noble man makes noble plans, and by noble deeds he stands" (Isaiah 32:8)

"If you don't make plans for yourself, someone else will make plans for you."
—Jim Rohn

The kind of *deeds you do* as a businessperson result from the kind of *plans you make*. And the kind of plans you make are determined by your character. Will you make wise plans, foolish plans, or no plans at all?

Noble is defined as "exalted moral character or excellence." Do your business plans serve a higher purpose than simply becoming rich and famous? Do your plans include treating your family like royalty? Do your plans reap or rape the "fields" from which you draw your profits? Do your plans please the King of kings in whose image you are made?

"In a large house there are articles not only of gold and silver, but also of wood and clay; some are for noble purposes and some for ignoble. If a man cleanses himself from the latter, he will be an instrument for noble purposes..." (2 Timothy 2:20-21).

Stop, think, dream, and pray.

"In his heart a man plans his course, but the Lord determines his steps"
(Proverbs 16:9).

Are you too busy "fighting alligators" that you don't have time to "drain the swamp"? Problem solving is great, but you must go beyond that if you want your business to grow. Planning is necessary to chart the course of your business' future. You must take the first step:

STOP what you're doing. Lay aside the problems for a day and get away. Find a place without distractions. A place where you can:

THINK about what you're doing, why you're doing it, how, etc. Is this what you want to be doing? Can you do it better? Where do you want to be in a year...five years? Then you're ready to:

DREAM about doing great things...making a better life for yourself and family...making a positive contribution to this world. Then:

PRAY for direction and resources to accomplish it all. Commit yourself and your business to the will of God.

Every glamorous business has its unglamorous side.

"By the sweat of your brow you will eat your food until you return to the ground, since from it you were taken" (Genesis 3:19).

The kind of business you start should flow naturally out of your own experience and giftings. Sometimes we ignore this preparation and try to fit into a "dream business" that seems more glamorous. But, all businesses have their down sides. (e.g., some may think advertising is a really glamorous business. In reality you work 70-80 hours a week; your creative ideas are often rejected by clients; and you usually need to have everything done "yesterday.") Don't let "apparent glamor" mislead you. Every business involves some "sweat."

What are you best suited for? You might want to prepare a personal inventory statement. This is a list of your skills, knowledge, talents, resources, contacts, hobbies, and other assets. Also consider your weaknesses. Do they disqualify you from being in business or can you fortify that area through diligent effort or by finding a partner or manager who complements your weak areas?

Identify your motivation for going into business.

"For the word of God is quick, and powerful, and sharper than any two-edged sword...and is a discerner of the thoughts and intents of the heart"
(Hebrews 4:12 KJV).

"**B**e your own boss" the ads promise, pandering to people's desire for independence. One statistic claims that 50% of adults are unhappy with their job or business. Perhaps they are unhappy with their boss or supervisor and yearn for freedom.

A major problem with the "be your own boss" mentality is that it just doesn't work that way in real life. The reality is that every business owner has to answer to somebody—actually a lot of somebodys—their customers, clients, patients, etc. How many "bosses" can you count now?

If you're not ready to answer to many people, taking the posture of a servant, it might be best to stick with *one* boss until you are.

Count the *hidden* costs of going into business.

"Suppose one of you wants to build a tower. Will he not first sit down and estimate the cost to see if he has enough money to complete it?"
(Luke 14:28).

Counting the cost of going into business is not just a matter of calculating start-up costs and operating expenses. The cost of starting a business also includes sacrificing time spent with family and friends. There may be many late nights put in at your desk or store. Is your family at a place where being away from them is feasible or desirable? You may need to be creative in carving out quality time with them. Are you good at juggling time to meet the needs that arise both at home and in your business? Does your family support your decision to be in business?

Do you feel support from members of your church? Do they understand the sacredness of the calling of being in business? Some may be critical of your lack of attendance at times.

It can help if you explain to family and friends how your business serves the purposes of God. Enlist their prayer support—believe me, you'll need it.

Make a commitment to succeed.

"You won't reach your full potential unless you understand total commitment."
—Heeth Varnedo, CEO, Flowers Industries

I remember well the commitment I made to myself and to God. I was driving down the road thinking about starting my own business. I had felt that God was leading me to do it, and was at the point of decision. In my dialogue with the Lord I said, "I'll sure try."

The Lord responded, "That's not good enough."

So I strengthened my stance, "I'll do my very best."

The answer: "That's still not good enough. You must make a *commitment* to succeed."

I was stunned, knowing instantly in that moment of revelation that there was no going back—that failure was not an option. That I would, indeed, not be able to do it on my own but have to rely on God's help. In the years that have followed, that commitment to succeed has carried us through some difficult times in our business. Without it we probably would have quit years ago. Because of it, we have just celebrated 13 years in business.

Your character is more important than your cause.

"But we also rejoice in our sufferings, because we know that suffering produces perseverance; perseverance, character; and character, hope"
(Romans 5:3-4).

Who you are is more significant than what you do. "Character" is the sum of your moral qualities and ethical standards. It can be insightful to sit down and write out a summary of the rules you live by and run your business by. Here are a few areas to consider:

1) What is my view of success and prosperity?
2) What responsibility do I have to others?
3) What is the philosophy that guides my business?
4) What things are "out of bounds" for my life?
5) What is the source of my mandate for business?
6) How do I relate to the Ten Commandments?
7) How do I relate to the Sermon on the Mount?

If you take as much time to consider the ramifications of your *moral* decisions as you do *financial* decisions, it will build your character. Ultimately, strong character will have a positive effect on your business.

Stay with what you do best.

"Do you see a man skilled in his work? He will serve before kings; he will not serve before obscure men" (Proverbs 22:29).

I had been in business 8 years when I got bit by the "retail" bug. Our advertising business was finally paying off, and I had some extra money to invest. Should I buy real estate or invest in a retail business? One of my mentors cautioned that he had seen too many businesses fail in which the investor/owner didn't know much about the industry they were getting into.

Trouble is, even with good advice, sometimes you only hear what you want to hear. I had a dozen reasons why this would work for *me*. So I jumped headfirst into the retail jewelry business. It's true I had learned a lot about managing a business—but that was a service business. I didn't really understand retail and I certainly didn't know jewelry.

A year and a half later I bailed out. We're still paying off the debt. We paid a high price to learn this lesson—it's something we won't easily forget.

Test your E.Q. (your entrepreneurship quotient).

"To one he gave five talents of money, to another two talents, and to another one talent, each according to his ability"
(Matthew 25:15).

If you are considering starting a business or have already done so but are not sure if you have the temperament for it, you might want to take this little test, adapted from *Success* magazine:

1) Can you handle loneliness? ☐ Yes ☐ No

2) Can you handle the pervasiveness of the business in your life? ☐ Yes ☐ No

3) Can you emotionally handle the risk of starting a business? ☐ Yes ☐ No

4) Can you accept the financial strain and physical drain of long hours? ☐ Yes ☐ No

5) Can you accept opposition and misunderstanding from friends and loved ones? ☐ Yes ☐ No

The more "yes" answers you have the better suited you are to being an entrepreneur. Of course you can be in business without being one, but it helps.

Two rules for getting more business: #1 be worthy; #2 ask.

"Well done, good and faithful servant! You have been faithful with a few things; I will put you in charge of many things" (Matthew 25:21).

Getting more business is a function of two important principles that, by themselves will work, but when combined are dynamite.

The most important prerequisite for getting more business is *being worthy* of more. If you haven't worked the "bugs" out of your product or service, don't try to grow. Work the problems out first. That way only a few people will know you don't have your act together. If you already have a quality product or service you still need to demonstrate staying power. Customers want to know if you're going to be around next year to service what you sell.

The second rule for getting more business is to simply *ask* for it. Ask your existing customers if there are other ways you can serve them. Ask them for referrals.

To get new customers, your advertising needs to communicate that you are ready, willing, and able to serve their needs.

Your most valuable asset is your existing customers.

"Old customers are the key to growth and profitability." —Jay Abraham

Many businesses spend more money trying to acquire new customers than they do to retain or increase sales to the ones they already have. It should be the other way around. One of the biggest hurdles in getting new customers is establishing trust. Trust is not easy to come by, but existing customers already have a certain amount of trust in your product or service.

When business starting slacking off with one of my major clients, I asked myself: "What else can I do to serve their needs?" I uncovered a few new areas in which I could be of service and soon revenues from them were up.

Ask yourself: How else can I serve my existing customers? Is there something else I can "cross-sell" to them related to what we're already doing? Then ask them: "What else can we provide?" If they've stopped buying from you, ask them why—without being defensive. You may be able to win them back.

Continually upgrade the value of your product or service.

"God saw all that He had made, and it was very good" (Genesis 1:31).

There are two kinds of value that you need to continually work at upgrading. The first is the *intrinsic value* of your product or service. Today, consumers are better educated and more informed about the quality of goods and services in the marketplace. If you don't grow with the times you'll be left in your competitor's dust.

Back in the early days of our business, we discovered that we didn't have some of the hardware and software that our competitors did. We "bit the bullet," made the investment, and determined to never let that happen again. We have had to continually upgrade our computers and programs, but it's been well worth it because of what it has enabled us to do for our clients.

In the same way you must pay attention to the *perceived value* of your products or services. You must create the perception of value (quality, desirability, user benefits, etc.) that you want to have identified with your business and communicate it through your sales staff and advertising.

Little clients can become big clients.

"It is like a mustard seed, which is the smallest seed you plant in the ground. Yet when planted, it grows and becomes the largest of all garden plants" (Mark 4:31-32).

Be careful how you treat little customers, clients, or patients. The "little old lady" who comes in for her oil change may be getting ready to buy a brand new car...hopefully from you, if you've treated her as a valuable customer. When your business is small, most of your customers will be small. But don't *think* small. Think "New York." When we were starting out, I told my partner to not do ads *as though* they'd only be seen in our hometown. "Do them as though they're for New York, and *some day* they will be seen in New York!" (Today that same former partner has a project that's being considered by a major film studio.)

Your customers' needs will grow, so you must be prepared to grow with them. Work on improving the *quality* of your services or products and not just increasing the *quantity* of their orders. When their "ship comes in," you'll be right there at the docks—helping them to unload!

Creatively brainstorm for new business ideas.

"Two are better than one...though one may be overpowered, two can defend themselves"
(Ecclesiastes 4:9,12).

What do you do when you need some fresh ideas to grow your business or need a new angle to solve an old problem? You brainstorm of course! If you've never conducted a brainstorming session, you're in for a treat.

PREPARATIONS: Define exactly what it is you want to accomplish and explain it to your "storm troops" ahead of time (they can be workers, or trusted friends or family). Provide comfortable seating, attach large sheets of paper to the walls, and have some non-bleeding markers ready.

SESSION: Get the ball rolling with a few seed ideas to break the ice. Write the ideas in large print on the walls as fast as they come. Let no one judge or evaluate any of them. Just let it flow while keeping on the subject at hand. The dynamic of many minds creates a synergy. One idea can trigger an unexpected one from another. You'll be surprised what can be accomplished in one of these sessions (and it does a lot for the people involved, too).

Don't sow all your seed in one field.

"Sow your seed in the morning, and at evening let not your hands be idle, for you do not know which will succeed..." (Ecclesiastes 11:6).

The business that relies on one major client or customer group for its success is doomed to have some very difficult times. Even the best customers go through economic cycles. Building up your customer base is like investing in mutual funds—if one stock goes down the others will balance it out. So, too, every business must constantly give themselves to acquiring new customers. (This does not contradict what I've said earlier about paying attention to existing customers—rather it balances that statement.)

In our early years we practiced this advice regularly but, later on, our largest customer got very busy with us. It was too tempting to ignore customer acquisition. Soon about 80% of our business was with this one customer. When an unexpected downturn hit their industry, our business plummeted. Getting new business became a priority again. We could have avoided much difficulty if we had continued to obtain new customers all along.

Don't argue with or offend your customers.

"An offended brother is more unyielding than a fortified city, and disputes are like the barred gates of a citadel" (Proverbs 18:19).

One of my best clients was really giving me "what for" because we had missed a deadline and hadn't followed their procedures to a "T." I let it get the best of me and anger rose up within me. Soon it was "all over the table and walls!" The two managers I was meeting with were stunned. I had crossed the line and insulted them.

Later my partner and I found ourselves sitting in front of their superiors. I let my partner do the talking (I still wasn't sure I wanted their business). He made Henry Kissinger seem surly by comparison. Soon we were back on track with this client. I apologized, took the original complaint to heart and made some changes in the way we handled their account. Mostly I changed my attitude toward them and viewed their ongoing demand for fast turnaround as an opportunity to grow personally and professionally. Now we actually welcome jobs with short fuses. (We get paid sooner!)

Protect your inventions, ideas, and trade secrets.

"So Delilah said to Samson, 'Tell me the secret of your great strength and how you can be tied up and subdued'" (Judges 16:6).

When I was in my early twenties, I was eager to launch a graphic design and advertising business. One of our first projects was to "pitch" a homebuilder. We designed ads and billboards for this potential client and presented them to the manager. He was impressed with our work and asked us to leave the sketches with him. We naively agreed. We also did not include a copyright notice on our work.

In a couple of weeks our layouts were returned with a "thanks, but no thanks." Two months later, ads and billboards almost identical to our designs began to appear around town. There was nothing we could do.

If you've written something, put a copyright notice on it before you show it to anyone. If you've invented something, get a non-disclosure, non-compete agreement before you show it to someone. As for trade secrets, don't reveal them to anyone! Your creative ideas are what make you valuable in the marketplace—guard them closely.

Don't grow too fast.

"It is not good to have zeal without knowledge, nor to be hasty and miss the way" (Proverbs 19:2).

Our business started in our dining room, but we were off to a fast start. Monthly billings exceeded our projections and by the end of the year we had an outside suite of offices and had taken on a new partner. Early the next year we had signed a lease on a 2,000 sq. ft. building. New clients kept coming on board and created a bottleneck: me. So I reluctantly delegated design work to hired staff. My job became less creative and more administrative. I was working more, enjoying it less, and making less. Our staff had grown to 13 people and I was busy keeping everyone else busy.

Then the summer slowdown hit. The partners cut their salaries, and just making payroll was a challenge. We fell behind with our vendors. We scrambled to cut costs but the dominoes were already falling. By the end of the year we had dissolved the partnership, broken our lease, and moved back into our dining room. *Our growth curve had outstripped our learning curve.* My advice: slow down and grow carefully!

Don't expand what's not working.

"Now listen, you who say, 'Today or tomorrow we will go to this or that city...carry on business and make money.' Why you do not even know what will happen tomorrow" (James 4:13-14).

One of the great benefits of starting a business small is that you can fine tune it while the cost of mistakes is also small. So many of us want to grow quickly and realize our dreams overnight. This happened to us with a retail jewelry kiosk we owned in one of the local shopping malls.

We opened the first one in April and were only marginally successful. We were "breaking even" but we still hadn't solved all of our inventory, accounting, and employee problems. As Christmas approached, we chomped at the bit to open two additional locations. We "went for it." But the lack of strength in our first kiosk couldn't bear the weight of additional problems at the second one.

We had to close #2 just as #3 was opening. We could have avoided a lot of difficulty if we had fine tuned the first one. On the other hand, when you have a properly functioning model, it's a lot easier to duplicate your success.

People are more important than things.

*"God is more interested in what He is doing in
you than what He can do through you."*
—Rich Worsham

The people involved in your business (you and your family, customers, employees and suppliers) are more important than the things it takes to keep your business ticking (goals, to-do lists, activities and even profits). When you think of your business, do you think of people or things (the product or service, your equipment and building, etc.)?

I read somewhere that "being in business is not about getting rich, but about becoming the person you were destined to be." Being in business is about God doing something inside you (perfecting leadership and servanthood). It's about caring more for people than the bottom line. Yes, you must show a profit to continue in business. But at what price? Must you lose your family ? Many have. Must you trample on others to be "successful"? Many do.

Someone once said that all of our activities are only "scaffolding." What God is really interested in is the "building." That building is people's lives.

Challenge your employees to grow.

"The fire will test the quality of each man's work. If what he has built survives, he will receive his reward" (1 Corinthians 3:13-14).

Think of your business as scaffolding, and your employees as the building. You have a responsibility to them, not only to provide a fair wage, but also to provide opportunities for them to be challenged and grow. In this age of tearing people down, do you find ways to encourage them? Do you trust them with problem-solving and creative tasks? Job security is not found in trying to remain indispensible; it is found in increasing the expertise and value of the whole team. Meet with each one on a regular basis to let them know specifically how you expect them to grow. Be careful not to stretch them too far, too fast. If you challenge your whole staff by precept and example, your company or practice will be known as a class act.

You must also challenge your staff members to work as a team. They must learn to value one another personally and as important contributors to the team effort. It's not the quarterback who wins the game—it's the whole team.

Cut the monkey business.

"For I myself am a man under authority, with sol-diers under me. I tell this one, 'Go,' and he goes; and that one 'Come,' and he comes" (Matthew 8:9).

What in the world is "monkey business?" I actually learned about "monkey business" a few years before I went into business. I had gone for training to prepare for the school I was about to start. "Monkey Business" I was told, was a part of a larger topic: "The Care and Feeding of Monkeys." No, I haven't flipped out. This is really going to be helpful to you.

The "monkey" thing is really a metaphor for delegating responsibility. When you delegate a responsibility, it's like giving a subordinate a monkey to feed. If the monkey is not fed, it might die and stink up the place. If a monkey handler is co-dependent they may be carrying around a lot of other people's monkeys on their back. If a monkey handler tries to give it back to the boss, you've got some *serious monkey business*. Using metaphors like these helps employees to see more clearly what you're trying to accomplish and the consequences of failure in their jobs.

Sack bad employees quickly.

"And throw that worthless servant outside, into the darkness, where there will be weeping and gnashing of teeth" (Matthew 25:30).

We had just opened our new jewelry kiosk. Traffic was high and we were sure we'd do well there. Because of the distance to the new location, it was difficult to check up on our employees daily. We trusted the manager of this location to operate our business with integrity and to report accurately. Before long, there was strife between this manager and the other employees. We tried to be patient with them as weeks dragged by.

Then we started noticing "shrinkage" in the inventory. We should have sacked these employees early on. Sales were so poor we had to close the location after two months. We assumed it was because our product didn't appeal to this market. The day we closed, other store clerks came by to tell us what had been going on. Our employees were known to treat customers rudely and even leave the kiosk unattended, making our product vulnerable to shoplifters. Sometimes the problem is not the product, but the staff.

Never go into a meeting unprepared.

"You cannot speak that which you do not know... Good communication starts with good preparation." —Treasury of Quotes by Jim Rohn, ©1994.

It is estimated that 50% of a corporate executive's time is spent in meetings. The small entrepreneur will also spend a significant amount of time in meetings. Whether a staff meeting or a meeting with a customer, you'd better be prepared to run the meeting smoothly, keep it on track, and finish with the desired objective.

Here are my rules for running an effective meeting:

1) Always be prepared. Never go into a meeting without an objective, an agenda, and ammunition. Even impromptu meetings should never be totally ad-lib. If you bump into someone you need to meet with, avoid the temptation to do so if you have not previously prepared for it.

2) Always state the purpose of the meeting up front so all participants will know what's expected.

3) Keep the discussion moving toward a conclusion.

4) Every meeting should end with some resolution or action items.

Beware
of "rogue" advice.

"Continue in what you have learned and have become convinced of, because you know those from whom you have learned it" (2 Timothy 3:14).

A rogue elephant can be extremely dangerous. He can become separated from the herd and can attack without provocation. Beware of would-be advisors who are *out of touch* with your life and know little of the areas in which they would advise you.

I've had my share of bad advice. It usually has come from people I didn't know. One gentleman advised me to expand a retail business into a certain location. We checked it out. It certainly was a busy location, but after we started up, we found it was very difficult to manage the business long distance. The result was disastrous.

I've also had lots of good advice—mostly from people who know me well. Some of the material in this book has come from relationships with trusted mentors. An advisor who knows *you* may be more important than one who knows *the field* but doesn't have a clue about your strengths and weaknesses.

Pray for your customers and suppliers.

"Do not be anxious about anything, but in everything, by prayer and petition...present your requests to God" (Philippians 4:6).

When you pray for God's blessing on your business (you should), do you forget to pray for your customers and suppliers? It's probably more critical that you pray for them to be blessed because *your* prosperity is contingent on *theirs*. One business does not make up an economy. Neither does one industry. We need a multitude of businesses and industries to make an economic system work.

One of the most important activities of your staff meetings should be to pray that your customers, clients, or patients will be blessed. Pray not only for their financial blessing but also that you will be more sensitive to their needs, and better able to serve them. Pray also for your vendors' and suppliers' prosperity. Pray for their protection as they seek to fill orders for resources critical to your own success.

Prayer is not one-dimensional. If you'll turn it outward you may find that it's more effective.

Don't use too sharp a pencil on your budgets.

" A prudent man foresees the difficulties ahead and prepares for them; the simpleton goes blindly on and suffers the consequences"
(Proverbs 22:3, *The Living Bible*).

"Why do I always run short of cash?" I asked my mentor. After a few moments he replied "Your pencil is too sharp." "What do you mean?" I asked. "What I mean is: when you do your budgets, you figure them down to the last penny but don't leave any room for contingencies."

I've often heard it said that a person's greatest strength is also their greatest weakness. My strength, in this case, was being very detailed in my planning. Conversely my weakness was in relying on the details to work out exactly as I had planned.

Don't get me wrong: I believe wholeheartedly in planning. What I needed to learn was how to *plan for the unexpected* to happen as well. Most consultants say to add 10-20% to your budget estimates. My perfectionist nature cringes at this idea but I know from experience it needs to be done.

Save for a dry and dusty day.

"Seven years of great abundance are coming throughout the land of Egypt, but seven years of famine will follow them..." (Genesis 41:29-30).

I'll never forget my reaction when I first heard a friend of mine share on the "Cycles of Prosperity" from the life of Joseph. As he explained, it's not a matter of *if* lean years will come but *when* will they come, and, will we be prepared.

Joseph instructed Pharaoh to store a portion of grain during the seven fat years. Then seven years of famine began. Not only was Egypt saved, but many foreign countries came to buy grain from them and were saved also.

My reaction on hearing this was: "Where were you when my business was doing well?" I had not been prepared for the downturn I was in and was hurting financially. I promised myself I would save during the next "up season." About a year later I had several thousand dollars in savings and was considering buying an expensive piece of equipment. Then I remembered the story of Joseph and decided to finance the purchase. Later that year another dry season hit but our savings carried us through.

Don't borrow from Peter's fund to pay Paul's expense.

"Do not say to your neighbor, 'Come back later; I'll give it tomorrow'—when you now have it with you" (Proverbs 3:28).

The early years of our business were fraught with many mistakes due to my inexperience and lack of wisdom. Most of the problems stemmed from improper money handling. My view of our finances was usually too optimistic.

When things got tight during our second summer, I saw no alternative but to take a check that was supposed to cover a printing bill and use it to pay other bills and meet payroll. Later, I had a problem coming up with enough money at one time to pay this rather large bill. Weeks went by; still no payment. Then a call from the printer: "Where's my money?" I made a lame excuse but silently wondered how I'd get out of this mess.

When the bill reached 90 days past due, I knew that normal cash flow was not going to solve the problem. I finally had to finance the payment of that bill. Since then we've made it a rule to use earmarked funds for their intended purpose only.

A dollar saved can be worth four dollars earned.

"A penny saved, is a penny earned."
—Benjamin Franklin

Cutting costs is one of the most efficient ways to add to your bottom line. Any direct or indirect costs (overhead) saved go *directly* to the bottom line. On the other hand, additional sales or revenues usually have some cost connected with them. Let's say you purchase an item for resale at a cost of $10. You mark it up 100% to sell at retail. So on this sale, you had to sell $20 to add $10 to your bottom line. That's without overhead or commissions figured in. Let's say your overhead is $5 on each $20 item sold. This means your profit is only $5 on a $20 sale.

When looking at it in this light, a $5 cut in costs can be worth the profit on a $20 sale—or to put it another way a dollar saved could be worth four dollars earned (sold). These numbers will vary depending on your particular business, and of course I've oversimplified to make a point. But the bottom line (pun intended) is: if money's tight, cut costs first.

Test
before you invest.

"Test everything. Hold on to the good"
(1 Thessalonians 5:21).

I'm an entrepreneur at heart. And one thing entrepreneurs enjoy most is starting new ventures. While I've focused most of my energy on our primary business, I've experimented with other sideline businesses. It's always been the sheer excitement of making it work. The novelty, the challenge—that's what is so exciting.

Somehow we got on an "opportunity seekers" mailing list. Now, there literally isn't a week that goes by that I don't get some money-making offer in the mail. One of these offers came in a card deck. "Best one-person business ever" it said. "Only $6995" it continued. I checked into it a bit more. It offered a turn-key business—pepper gas, personal defense spray—with inventory, territory and 30 locations set up for me. I thought: "Maybe I should buy some of this product from another supplier and see if it will sell in our area."

Instead I went for the "turn-key" approach. The product didn't sell. I should have tested before I invested $6995!

Investigate *before* you test.

"Caveat emptor" (Let the buyer beware!).
—Anonymous

Another one of my ill-fated ventures involved a "discount music coupon book" that was designed to be sold to organizations as a fundraising device. I called the Better Business Bureau in the company's hometown—no complaints there. Next I called one of their distributors in another part of the country. He was having great success selling the coupon books. What else could I have done to check them out? I could have purchased a coupon book from their distributor and tried ordering music myself. I might have visited their home office in an adjoining state. I wish I had. Before I had a chance to hit the streets with my $2300 worth of coupon books (my cost), I found out the company had declared bankruptcy.

A big part of the problem in starting a business with someone else's product or method is that your success is dependent on their success. If they go under, can you buy the product from the manufacturer? If not, the venture is like a time bomb, waiting to explode in your face.

Make the most of the 80/20 rule.

"The secret of the wealthy is time management."
—Brian Tracy, author and speaker

There is a rule of thumb in business that says: 80% of your results (or profit) are produced by 20% of your efforts (or time). Conversely, 20% of your results *consume* 80% of your time. Your numbers may vary from this rule, but the principle holds true: all parts of your business are not equally profitable. Time spent getting new customers, managing employees, etc. is "overhead." These are necessary but nevertheless "non-billable" pursuits. The things you do that you are actually paid for probably consume a smaller proportion of your time. This seems inefficient.

Here's what I've tried to do to remedy this in my business: I'm constantly looking for ways to reduce "overhead time" by simplifying or eliminating unproductive activities. At the same time I try to increase my percentage of "billable" or paying activities. I know this has worked because I've been able to generate about the same amount of annual revenues with one-sixth of the number of employees that we used to have.

Keep your accounts receivable on a short leash!

"The wicked borrow and do not repay"
(Psalm 37:21).

Quite often going into *any* sort of business also means going into the "banking" business. Sooner or later you'll have to offer payment terms. At some point in the transaction you'll have to decide if the customer is credit worthy. Get references (at least 3) as a routine procedure (that way no one is offended) and check them out. Another bit of insurance is to get a deposit up front, if appropriate. This can weed out the "deadbeats" in advance. (This also must apply to friends. It helps them plan their orders more carefully and keeps the deal on a professional level.) To encourage early payment, offer a discount of 2%.

Once you have extended credit, make sure they understand your terms and late payment penalties. If their check hasn't arrived on time, call or send a copy of the bill stamped "past due" with the late charges added. If there's no response then send a letter, and as a last resort offer an installment plan or a deadline after which it will be turned over to a collection agency.

Don't buy until the need is evident.

"And the wise heart will know the proper time and procedure...for every matter"
(Ecclesiastes 8:5-6 NIV).

When we first started our advertising business we had two computers but couldn't afford a laser printer (this was 10 years ago when they cost $5000—today the equivalent printer is under $500). Since the whole point of our business was recording our ideas on paper we needed a decent output device. A dot-matrix printer wouldn't do.

After a little research we found a local printer who was willing to print our pages for 50¢ each. That was cheap enough, but it usually took 2 hours to travel there, print the pages, and return home. This was okay when we only had to make one or two trips a week (it would be a nightmare now—totally unthinkable in today's instant fax era). When it got to be a daily affair it was time to invest in the laser printer. But we didn't make the purchase until the need was evident. Equipment that gathers dust usually indicates an unwise purchase. And not investing—when the time has come to buy—is just as foolish.

Charge the "going rate"–you're worth it!

"For the scripture saith, 'Thou shalt not muzzle the ox that treadeth out the corn.' And, 'The labourer is worthy of his reward'" (1 Timothy 5:18 KJV).

I once asked a friend, who is a financial planner, to review our insurance, investments, and financial goals. He sat before me with his laptop cranking out charts and projections. We got to talking about cash flow and the hourly rates I was charging. His response: "You're worth more than that. You should be charging more." The figure he mentioned was double what I was charging at the time. His statement increased the perceived value of my time by a factor of two.

I began charging that rate, and to my surprise no one objected. I was selling myself short. Later, I learned that I needed to charge four times what I actually needed to "draw" out since only half my hours were billable and half of the revenues went to overhead. A footnote: a few months ago I talked with a young friend in the recording business. I told him he was worth four times what he was charging. He took it to heart. Now he actually gets up to eight times his original hourly rate. But you know what? He's worth it!

Work with a good accountant.

"The Lord abhors dishonest scales, but accurate weights are His delight"
(Proverbs 11:1).

When you're starting a business or running a small business (with just yourself or a few employees) you usually have to wear more than one hat. Maybe you're the sales force, the service provider or manufacturer, and perhaps the office manager, too. But there's one area where it just doesn't pay to avoid using an outside professional. Unless balance sheets, P & L's, and the IRS Tax code are second nature to you, retain a good CPA to keep your finances on track.

By all means, do the bookkeeping (write checks, keep up with accounts receivable and payable, make entries in a general ledger or computer program) but leave the balance sheets and tax returns to a pro. It will save you a lot of grief (and sometimes money, too, since they know how to help you structure your business to take advantage of any tax breaks). They are great at helping you avoid penalties and keeping you on track with Uncle Sam.

Pay your taxes as you go.

"This is also why you pay taxes, for the authorities are God's servants, who give their full time to governing" (Romans 13:6).

During our first year in business, we somehow failed to realize that we needed to be making estimated tax payments. When the following March rolled around and we got our tax return back from the accountant, we were shocked! We didn't have $5,000 laying around. We decided to borrow the money to pay Uncle Sam. Three years later we made our final payment on that loan.

In our second year of business I had to make payments for the previous year's tax as well as estimated payments for the current year. The problem was that my tax bill was higher than expected and we wound up short again. This time our reserves were depleted. We struggled and managed to make the payments by the grace of God.

This year we're finally up to date. But I sure wish we had gotten off on the right foot from the very beginning.

Pay employees first, creditors second, yourself last.

"Finish your outdoor work and get your fields ready; after that, build your house"
(Proverbs 24:27).

Few business owners are sometimes mistaken about how they view their businesses. They think of it as a job and that they are entitled to a larger weekly paycheck. Since they are working harder than when they worked for someone else, they feel they are entitled to make more than before. In this scenario, employees, if there are any, get paid second, and vendors get paid last if there's anything left over. The problem with the "pay myself first" mentality is that it takes the edge off proper financial management. Ultimately it means big trouble for the business.

Pay your employees first, if you have any. Without them your operation could come to a grinding halt. You also have a responsibility to help support their families. Next pay your creditors—banks first, then vendors. Is there enough left to pay yourself? Now the pressure is where it belongs. You'll do a better job of selling and/or managing when you're in this position.

43

Render to Caesar and to God.

"Bring the whole tithe into the storehouse....'Test me in this,' says the Lord Almighty, 'And see if I will not...pour out so much blessing that you will not have room enough for it'" (Malachi 3:9-10).

Many believe that free enterprise is the secret of America's prosperity. What I'd like to suggest is that the principle of "rendering" is the secret of our strength.

First, *render* to Caesar. One year we thought we had taken out enough taxes through our estimated tax payments, but had made an error and needed to pay $14,000 in just 2-1/2 months. We put this before the Lord and continued to do the second part of today's statement—we continued to *render* to God (tithe). We figured out how much we needed to put aside each week for taxes and somehow every week we were able to do it until April 15 came and we had the entire amount!

I firmly believe God helped us do it. Every time we wrote a tithe check my wife prayed, "We're testing you Lord!" I still don't know exactly "how" we did it, but I do know we couldn't have done it on our own.

Lessons you learn with your own money endure, but the tuition is high.

"Instruct a wise man and he will be wiser still; teach a righteous man and he will add to his learning" (Proverbs 9:9).

You'll learn many lessons in your business first hand which you'll not easily forget. You can also learn from the mistakes of others. Those lessons are a lot less costly. Here's a list of additional lessons I've learned "in the fire":

1) Establish a waiting period for all major purchases. 2) Wait a day before you sign any contract. 3) Don't pay for information you can get free. 4) Don't overbuy inventory or run out of inventory. 5) The best investment you can make is in your own business. 6) Avoid hiring until it really hurts business. 7) Don't spend more than you take in. 8) Don't borrow more than you can pay back. 9) Make each department or product pay its own way. 10) When money gets tight—start pruning. 11) Buy supplies as you need them—don't stockpile. 12) Make a budget and stick to it. 13) If you're not using something—quit storing it. 14) Don't brag about how well you're doing financially. 15) Don't wear yourself out getting rich.

Chart your progress and record your milestones.

"This is the day you are to commemorate; for the generations to come you shall celebrate it as a festival to the Lord—a lasting ordinance"
(Exodus 12:14).

Do you record the activities of your business—not just for tax purposes, but for historical reasons as well? What is the history of your business? How did it get started? What were your hopes and dreams for it? How much progress have you made thus far?

Creating charts or graphs of sales growth can be both a diagnostic tool and pat on the back for a job well done. You can create plaques to document recognition of employees' achievement.

Create a photographic record of your history: your beginnings, your growth, your achievements. Take advantage of photo opportunities with dignitaries, company parties and picnics, community involvement, and so on.

If you haven't already done so, it's not too late to start now.

You are the shepherd of your business.

"Be sure you know the condition of your flocks...the lambs will provide you with clothing...you will have plenty of goats' milk to feed you and your family..." (Proverbs 27:23-27).

This is what I call the agricultural model of business management: each facet of your business is like a little flock. All flocks need shepherds. Without them the flock tends to stray.

Your staff is a flock, they need your constant supervision and direction. Your finances are a flock: don't just entrust them to your accountant—look after them on a regular basis. Your inventory is a flock: is it healthy? Your suppliers are a flock: have they strayed from your specifications? Even your customers are a flock!

Check these flocks out on a regular basis. Figuratively run your hands over them to make sure they haven't picked up burrs or are bleeding. Do they need greener pastures? Only the wise "shepherd" can tell.

Obey your internal traffic signals.

"After the earthquake came a fire, but the Lord was not in the fire. And after the fire came a gentle whisper" (1 Kings 19:11-12).

Here's an insight that comes from my wife, Kathy. We were looking back on some of our failed sideline businesses (the ones we experimented with, other than our primary business). Why hadn't they worked? Didn't we have God's direction and blessing? Nevertheless many of these attempts to add "multiple income streams" had failed miserably. The lessons were costly; we felt guilty about wasting resources.

Kathy had this comment: "You know, when we asked for divine guidance about these business ventures, we never had a 'red light' indicating we should *not* proceed. But neither did we get a clear 'green light' either, indicating a 'this is the way, walk ye in it' mandate to proceed."

I can only conclude that God *let* us do it, *not led* us to do it: those failed efforts were a response to *human possibility* and not *divine purpose*. Now we are determined to wait for the green light because we need to build our businesses on the calling and will of God.

Keep it simple.

"There are only about a half dozen things that make 80% of the difference in any area of our lives." —Jim Rohn

I have always been drawn to the idea of simplicity. Some of my favorite books growing up were in the "made simple" series. (*Physics Made Simple, Writing Made Simple*, etc.). No one today will deny that life has gotten very complicated. And being in business can be mind boggling. A return to simplicity is needed. Do you need balance in your life? There are about a half dozen things to pay attention to: Your family, your health, your spirituality, your finances, your business, and your social life.

Want to know if your business is financially on track? Again there are about a half dozen things to pay attention to: cash in the bank, A/P vs A/R, receipts vs. expenses for each month, projected revenues or work-in-process, year-to-date numbers vs. last year's numbers, and total debt.

Some people insist on *over*-organizing or *over*-administrating their lives and businesses. They may find some *security* in that approach, but miss out in *satisfaction*.

Small changes can produce big results.

"Catch for us the foxes, the little foxes that ruin the vineyards..." (Song of Songs 2:15).

The "little foxes" have a nasty habit of showing up just before harvest time. Sometimes they are difficult to spot until the damage is done. The real problem is that just a few of these little critters can spoil the whole harvest (put you out of business). We tend to ignore these little creatures, thinking they can't do much harm. Until it's too late.

How do little foxes manifest themselves in your "vineyard"? They could be little details you overlook (details that are important to your customers). They could appear as errors in bookkeeping during your busy season that can hold some nasty surprises. Or they could be employees slacking off.

In my advertising business, I have the opportunity to consult with a lot of people who are starting up or who are trying to turn their business around. The thing I've noticed is how close they sometimes are to a workable marketing plan. Often just a small change in their formula will produce the success they are working for.

Don't kick the broom!

"He that is slow to anger is better than the mighty; and he that ruleth his spirit than he that taketh a city" (Proverbs 16:32 KJV).

"Kicking the broom" has become sort of a code phrase with us that refers to losing your temper. It came from an incident that happened years ago. My wife was having a problem with something and she was also having a problem talking about it. This made me angry. (It didn't take much back then.) It escalated to the point where I was fuming mad so I kicked the kitchen broom down the stairs. Later I learned that my wife was trying to ask me a question about how to have patience with the neighbor children. How ironic.

Since then, I've "seen the light" about my anger, but not before I had given my wife gastritis (similar to an ulcer). One thing I've learned about anger: it tends to stifle your business growth. Why should God give you more business if you can't calmly handle the problems that come with the business you already have?

New computer?
This means war!

*"For our struggle is not against flesh and blood,
but against the...the spiritual forces of evil
in the heavenly realms"* (Ephesians 6:12).

I don't know how it is in your office or shop, but whenever we get a new computer or piece of software, there's a battle to tame it and make it do our bidding. I suppose that's one reason why I tend to delay such purchases.

Probably the biggest battle that ever raged in our office revolved around the most expensive printer we ever purchased. We bought an imagesetter "used" from an out-of-state company. I wanted to save some money so I didn't purchase a service contract (mistake!). Then the problems began. Six months and about $2000 later the machine was still not working. I finally broke down and bought a service contract (another $3500).

On the next service call, the technician decided it needed a new hard drive and motherboard. Voilá! Problem solved. In hindsight I realize I wasn't battling a machine or the guy I bought it from, but forces of discouragement and despair that came against me.

"Picture"
your success.

"Now faith is the substance of things hoped for,
the evidence of things not seen"
(Hebrews 11:1 KJV).

"Picturing" can be a very powerful motivating tool that can help you to reach your goals. I'm not talking about chanting, mantras, or any of that weird stuff. What I'm talking about is picturing in your mind some goal or dream connected to the fulfillment of your purpose. When you reach your goal, what will it look like? Find a photograph or drawing that represents your goal and post it where you can see it daily.

One of the dreams I've had most of my adult life is to have a cabin in the woods. When I was in art school I painted a picture of that little cabin. I've kept it through the years as a reminder of our own need to get away from the business, have some fun and relaxation, and have a place where we can write without interruptions and invite others to go to get refreshed also. What does *your* dream look like?

Maintain an attitude of gratitude.

"In America, success is easy—in Bangladesh it's hard." —Jim Rohn

In America, even the lowest on the economic ladder has it better than the poor of the world. It is estimated that one in five people in the world are so poor that their very survival is at stake on a daily basis. Two out of five human beings are malnourished. One and a half billion people don't have any health care. I could list a dozen other statistics each just as bleak and heartbreaking.

America, on the other hand, is still the richest country in the world. It is the "land of opportunity." Without being brilliant, or strong, or well-born, any American can rise from poverty and obscurity to achieve just about anything they set their mind and heart to do.

The next time you're feeling depressed about things in your business not going quite as well as you planned—remember, things are a lot worse for a great number of people in the world. So season your life with an attitude of gratitude.

Remember to *forget* past mistakes.

"Forgetting what is behind and straining toward what is ahead, I press on toward the goal..."
(Philippians 3:13-14).

As you have probably noticed, I've made plenty of mistakes in business. But I always try to put these failures behind me. Am I contradicting myself? Isn't this book a record of mistakes and misdeeds? No—it's a *record of lessons learned*. Don't ever forget the lessons you learn through your mistakes. What you need to let go of and *forget* is the pain and disappointment of errors large and small. Let go of the fear of failing again. Forgive yourself too!

Forgive the offenses that others commit against you. Don't hold grudges; don't get a chip on your shoulder. You never know when a former business enemy might be the only one who can help you: We were sued by one vendor (unjustly we felt), and had to pay a judgment in small claims court. At the time, I said things I later regretted and eventually wound up apologizing. A couple of years later this person came into a new relationship with the Lord and gave us $1000 when we really needed it!

The Businessperson's 23rd Psalm

The Lord is my mentor
I shall not flounder.
He shows me where opportunities lie.
He leads me to safe havens.
He restores my hope.
Though I walk through the
valley of disappointment,
danger and despair,
I will fear no failure
For He is with me.
His expert direction and training
brings me security.
He presents my greatest lessons
In the midst of the chaos around me.
He affirms my personal worth
And I'm filled with confidence.
Surely growth and maturity will mark my life
All the days we are associated.
And I will be His friend and partner forever.

"The plans of the diligent lead to profit"

(Proverbs 21:5).

"**D**iligence" is defined as a "constant and earnest effort to accomplish what is undertaken" (*The American College Dictionary*). I suppose it's only coincidental that I'm writing these words at midnight, but diligence sometimes requires burning the late-night oil. Diligence means doing whatever you have to do to get the job done. But diligence is more than a heroic effort to meet a deadline. The key word in our definition is "constant." That implies a steady pacing of effort. The picture that comes to mind is a marathon runner rather than a sprinter. In order to cover long distances, you've got to pace yourself at a sustainable rate.

Diligence is also "earnest." That means you take your responsibilities seriously. It means you work through the obstacles and hurdles that constantly seem to get in your way of finishing the job. Diligence is hanging in there when you feel like giving up. *Now put this kind of diligence together with planning and you've got the makings of success.*

To keep reaping, keep sowing.

"Remember this: whoever sows sparingly will also reap sparingly, and whoever sows generously will also reap generously" (2 Corinthians 9:6).

If you can't sleep at night and turn on the T.V., you're bound to hear a few pitches from the "I was broke but now I'm a millionaire" guys. One of their promises is that with their "secret information" you won't have to work hard and you can put your income on "automatic pilot." Now I'm not arguing with the reality of residual income—people who receive royalties or commission overrides do make money. What I am saying is that if neglected, any business will dwindle. Attrition will eventually eat away at your revenues.

Consider what I call the "agricultural model of marketing." When a farmer puts his seed in the ground he can expect a harvest in the fall. If he fails to replant the next spring, come fall the harvest will drop dramatically. No, he must keep sowing his seed if he intends to keep reaping. You must keep selling (and you must keep managing) if you expect to continue making money from your business.

Add *value* to all you do or produce.

"Dishonest money dwindles away, but he who gathers money little by little makes it grow"
(Proverbs 13:11).

The idea behind being a "value-added reseller" is that a retailer doesn't just move products from manufacturer to consumer. Instead he also provides "added value" by demonstrating and recommending products, and handling repairs and service in-house, among other things.

The "value added" concept should not be limited to retailers, however. Consider the publishing industry: the paper mill adds value to the raw pulp. Printers add value to the blank sheets of paper. Writers and artists add value to the ideas and images surrounding them when they bring these together to create a new book. The bookstore adds value to the finished product by recommending and making it available to the people who need this information.

The cycle doesn't end there. Readers of these books combine this information with their own ideas to produce better products and give better service. The more value you add to your product or service, the more you will sell.

Honesty is *still* the best policy.

"The integrity of the upright guides them, but the unfaithful are destroyed by their duplicity"
(Proverbs 11:3).

Honesty is very critical to your business and personal success. It is the foundation of all relationships. Without it we would have chaos in the marketplace. To be sure, there is deception in the bedroom and in the boardroom. But when it is exposed, as it inevitably will be, it brings ruin.

Honesty is the essence of communicating with integrity. We must demand honesty in all of our personal and business relationships. Our advertising must be truthful. We must pay the taxes we owe. We must not promise customers what we can't deliver. We must honor the commitments we have made—both verbal and in writing. We must also be honest with ourselves about what we expect of our business and what we're willing to give in return. Some Christians have a bad reputation in the marketplace—when it should be the reverse. Because of shoddy work and slow payment of bills, our testimony suffers. Let us determine to change that, wherever we live, to bring glory to the Lord.

MLM–it's not a lazy man's way to riches!

*"Lazy hands make a man poor,
but diligent hands bring wealth"*
(Proverbs 10:4).

MLM—Multi Level Marketing—has gained acceptance and legitimacy in the marketplace during recent years. Gone are the days of photocopied flyers and compensation plans. Most MLM companies today present their programs with full-color brochures and professionally produced videos.

Can MLM programs really produce huge incomes? For some, yes. But the average representative only makes about $100 a month. To achieve a significant income you need quite a number of people in your "downline."

Through the years I've gotten into several of these programs thinking that my upline, or my downline, would do all the work for me. The truth is, I wasn't prepared to make the kind of commitment required to be successful. If you want to get involved in network marketing be prepared to work and be prepared to stay with it. Success won't come overnight.

Keep a journal of business ideas and lessons learned.

"Then the Lord said to Moses, 'Write this on a scroll as something to be remembered'"
(Exodus 17:14).

This book has been developed from the notes I've kept about being in business. It's based on lessons I've learned and concepts I've read about and implemented. The process of remembering the pain of difficult lessons has been somewhat therapeutic for me. Looking back, I'm now able to view many of the events with a deeper perspective and understanding. I'm also better able to see how much I've learned and grown, and that is very satisfying. I would encourage you to keep a journal or notebook in which you can jot down seminal ideas that come to you, quotes you want to remember, and the lessons you're learning along the way. If it's been a while since you started your business, you can go back and reconstruct much of it from memory. The rest you can get from your spouse, business associates, and friends. It will be a valuable resource for your own review and for those with whom you share it.

Know what your competition is up to.

"To search out a matter is the glory of kings"
(Proverbs 25:2).

Do you enjoy being a sleuth? Do you have a means for gathering "intelligence" (as in C.I.A.) about your competitors and industry? Are you aware of soon-to-be-released technology that could revolutionize your field? Some of your best "market research" is learning what your competitors are up to. I'm not talking about illegally paying for secrets. I'm talking about keeping your eyes and ears open to what's going on around you.

What are your competitor's charging for similar services or products? Go and visit their location, call and ask for pricing (or have a friend or relative do this for you). What products or services are they offering?

What new products or technology are coming down the road? Subscribe to the top trade publications in your field.

How do customers view what your competitors are doing? Talk to them either formally as in a phone survey, or informally, just by asking around. Sometimes your competitors themselves will even give you the information.

Study the "Proverbs of Prosperity."

"I, wisdom, dwell together with prudence...with me are riches and honor, enduring wealth and prosperity" (Proverbs 8:12, 18).

Much wisdom can be found in the book of Proverbs for your life and business. You should make a habit of regularly studying Proverbs and in particular the "Proverbs of Prosperity" as a friend of mine calls them. Years ago he had studied Proverbs to find out what it had to say about prosperity. He collected all the verses in a booklet form. We often took one of those verses and discussed it during staff meetings, and then prayed that God would enable us to experience it in our lives.

The "Proverbs of Prosperity" are far too numerous to list here and it would do you more good to identify them for yourself. Every chapter of Proverbs contains one or more of these enlightening verses. And with 31 chapters in the book, you can read a different one each day of the month. Why not discover what treasures God has in store for you by reading Proverbs?

Never stop learning about your field.

"For each $1 you invest in yourself, you'll get $30 back."
—Brian Tracy

Whatever your field of endeavor, be it plumbing or plastic surgery, selling or sanitation, you can always learn more. The more you learn, the more you'll earn, too. If you want to be the best at what you do (and you should) you need to reinvest at least 3% of your income in continuing education. There are many resources available to you. These include books, trade publications, tapes, videos, seminars, workshops, classroom studies, trade shows, and meetings of your local trade association.

Whether it's technology or marketing techniques, every professional, businessperson, or tradesman needs to continuously learn more about what they do. There's an old saying: "Readers are leaders." Being in business is about being a leader.

Besides studying your own field, you should also be well-read in other areas of interest or avocation. It will make you a more interesting person.

Consider the sayings of those who've gone before.

Ponder these words from a former U.S. President.

You cannot bring about prosperity
by discouraging thrift.
You cannot strengthen the weak
by weakening the strong.
You cannot help the wage earner
by pulling down the wage payer.
You cannot further the brotherhood of man
by encouraging class hatred.
You cannot help the poor
by destroying the rich.
You cannot establish sound security
on borrowed money.
You cannot keep out of trouble
by spending more than you earn.
You cannot build character and courage
by taking away man's initiative and independence.
You cannot help men permanently by doing for them
what they would and should do for themselves.

—Abraham Lincoln (1859)

Enjoy these 20 fringe benefits of the righteous. *Psalm 37*

1) God will give us the desires of our heart (v. 4).
2) He will give us favor in people's eyes (v. 6).
3) We will inherit the land (v. 9).
4) We will enjoy great peace (v. 11).
5) God will protect us from the wicked (v. 15).
6) He will uphold us & give us strength (v. 17).
7) Our inheritance will endure (v. 18).
8) He will see us through disaster (v. 19).
9) We'll not starve in famine (v. 19).
10) We'll have plenty to give (v. 21).
11) If we stumble, we'll not fall (v. 24).
12) Our children will be blessed (v. 26).
13) We will live securely (v. 27).
14) We will utter wisdom (v. 30).
15) We will have a future (v. 37).
16) God will save us (v. 39).
17) He will be our refuge in time of trouble (v. 39).
18) He will help us (v. 40).
19) He will deliver us (v. 40).
20) We will be safe (v. 40).

Don't lose your family on the way to finding your success.

"A greedy man brings trouble to his family…"
(Proverbs 15:27 NIV).

Does your business require you to travel out of town a lot? Does it demand a lot more than 40 hours per week? Welcome to the club. Starting and running a business can be very draining on your time and energy. When you arrive home are you too tired to spend some quality time with your family? Do you always give the best hours of your day to your business, and what's left over to your family? If your family feels you don't care about them, they'll soon look elsewhere to get their needs met. Then you've lost them.

When a large number of successful executives and CEOs were surveyed, the one thing they regretted more than anything was not spending more time with their family. Why can people who are so successful in business fail so miserably at home? Clearly it's a matter of priorities. If you really want to do it, you *will* find the time. Learn to channel your creativity and problem-solving skills toward spending more time with your family—they're worth it!

Are you having fun yet?

"A man can do nothing better than to eat and drink and find satisfaction in his work...to the man who pleases Him, God gives wisdom, knowledge, and happiness" (Ecclesiastes 2:24, 26).

The phone was ringing off the hook, I had several appointments scheduled for the day, and I was trying to figure out when I'd work in some creative (billable) time. My partner poked his head into my office and with an encouraging smile asked: "Are you having fun?"

I responded: "Are we making any money?" But under my breath I muttered: "John's right, I've got to lighten up."

A real opportunity to do so came a few months later when a local TV news program asked a favor of our company. It was "National Goof Off Day" (seriously) and they needed to do a segment. We had two hours to prepare. Soon the video crew was at our door. Our receptionist was blowing bubbles, John was in the middle of an "engineering project" (train set), my wife was playing computer games, and our recording studio guys came up with a goof-off rap song. And you know what, we still got all our work done.

Are you having fun yet? (Part deux)

"In vain you rise early and stay up late, toiling for food to eat—for He grants sleep to those He loves" (Psalm 127:2).

One of the fun things about working in an office at home is that you've got a lot more opportunities to take breaks or get a snack from the kitchen. Kathy, my wife and partner, enjoys taking a break by going outside and checking on the "guys" (plants) in the garden. I enjoy walking over to her office and giving her a big hug.

A home office has its "dark side" though—sometimes we're still working after dark. The end of our workday is sometimes blurry. That's one of the reasons we have "date night." At 5 p.m. on Friday we shut down, no matter how busy we are. We go out to eat and enjoy being together. We also try to schedule weekend trips out of town every couple of months when finances permit. At one point we found we were working 7 days a week and still behind. That's when we decided to take weekends off as much as possible. They say work expands to fill the amount of time available. Now we still get the work done—only more efficiently.

Live long enough to enjoy the fruit of your labors.

"When God gives any man wealth and posses-sions, and enables him to enjoy them—to accept his lot and be happy in his work—that is a gift of God" (Ecclesiastes 5:19).

"**D**o not wear yourself out to get rich" says Proverbs 23:4. There have been weeks when I literally have worked night and day to meet my deadlines. The additional income of busy seasons can't really compensate for the physical and emotional wear and tear. When it occurs occasionally, beyond your control, it is tolerable. To plan for that kind of round-the-clock work is just plain crazy. It would be a shame to make all that money and not live to enjoy some of it or see it sown into the kingdom of God.

What kind of shape are you in physically? Do you get enough exercise and rest? Do you eat sensibly? Do you practice moderation? How's your weight? Do you take vita-mins?

Are you an emotional powderkeg? Do you have stress-relieving activities? Most major illnesses are stress related. If you don't take care of your health for yourself, do it for your loved ones—they want to enjoy that fruit *with* you.

71

Learn to avoid emotional extremes.

*"Like a city whose walls are broken down
is a man who lacks self-control"*
(Proverbs 25:28).

I had just gotten a call—a referral from one of my existing clients. This potential customer was getting ready to launch a new product and would need an extensive array of advertising materials. It was to be the single largest bid we had ever written. I was in ecstasy—this account would put us on the map. I told everyone I saw about it. In my mind it was a done deal and the coffers were already starting to look full. I hadn't learned this lesson yet: Don't get too excited when good news comes—things usually aren't as good as they *first* seem.

You guessed it, the bubble burst and I plunged into a "blue funk." It took a couple of days to recover after I found out we didn't get the project.

On the other hand, the reverse is also true: Don't be too upset with bad news—things usually aren't as bad as they *first* seem.

God didn't call us to be successful, He called us to be obedient!

"To obey is better than sacrifice" (1 Samuel 15:22 NIV).

My new publishing business was not doing well. I had assumed that I would be able to easily transfer my success in advertising and marketing into this new venture. It's true that I had learned many valid principles, but I would come to understand that applying them to a new field would take a lot more courage, diligence, faith and strength than I thought I had.

I felt like giving up on numerous occasions, wondering why I had ever left the lucrative field of advertising. I felt a bit like the Israelites after leaving the comfort of Egypt to wander 40 years in the wilderness.

Then the Lord reminded me that He had definitely and specifically called me into publishing. He impressed upon me that He had called me to be obedient, not successful. For awhile I kept thinking, "I'll be obedient, and then the success will come." But the Lord helped me to see that I was missing the point: True success is living in obedience to Him!

We learn ten times as much when the going is tough than when it's easy.

"Consider it pure joy, my brothers, whenever you face trials of many kinds, because you know that the testing of your faith develops perseverance. Perseverance must finish its work so that you may be mature and complete, not lacking anything" (James 1:2-4 NIV).

I've sort of adopted the above verse from James as my personal slogan for the past year. When it came to trials, I sure had a lot to "consider." Seriously though, I've been constantly encouraged this past year since the Lord brought this verse into focus for me.

The year of 1998 was one of the most difficult ones I've ever faced. When it was over I said, "Thank God that's over with." Then in early 1999 I started reading in the book of James and verse two hit me with full force. The Lord said, "You've got it all wrong about 1998. You were getting My best shots at character building. You ought to be rejoicing about that year because it will go down in history as one of your most beneficial years!"

Be faithful with the acre God has given you.

"'Well done, good and faithful servant! You have been faithful with a few things; I will put you in charge of many things'" (Matthew 25:21).

Some of the metaphors I've used in this book draw on my experiences of living and working on farms in Minnesota and Wisconsin. So I suppose it's only natural for me to hear from God in a form that is familiar to me.

When the Lord spoke to me about being faithful with the business He had given, He used the metaphor of an acre. He said, "I've given you an acre. If you'll be faithful with it, I'll give you another. There is no limit to the numbers of acres I'll give you, if you'll continue to be faithful."

Three important truths are implied in this promise from God: 1) The acre I started with came from God and it is really *His* acre—I'm just tending it for Him. 2) Faithfulness on my part is the key to the increasing responsibilities of more land. 3) Only God knows how many acres I'll wind up with, so I need to quit limiting what I think God is going to do.

God loves "pip-squeak" publishers.

"A bruised reed he will not break, and a smolder-ing wick he will not snuff out" (Isaiah 42:3 NIV).

One day I happened to be visiting a large discount chain store when I stopped to check out the Christian books that were being offered for sale. I noticed quite a number of well-known authors: Max Lucado, Phillip Yancey, Billy Graham, among others.

(Our publishing company had been trying to get this chain to carry some of our books. We presented some of our books to them, but none were selected for sale.)

So, on this particular day, when I stopped to see what kind of books they were offering, I realized that we were just a small blip on the publishing screen. As I walked away, somewhat discouraged, I said to the Lord, "I guess I'm just a pip-squeak publisher." The Lord responded, "Yes, but I love you pip-squeak!" Tears filled my eyes as I realized I hadn't missed what really counts in life: the approval of the Lord.

P.S. Several months later we received word that one of our titles would be offered through another large chain!

The seven deadly sins will rob you of your power to create wealth.

"You rebuke and discipline men for their sin; you consume their wealth like a moth" (Psalm 39:11 NIV).

What is the power to create wealth? I believe it is living in a way that both invites the blessing of God and eliminates the drains that rob us of what we already have. The "seven deadly sins" are so called because they can kill us spiritually. I also believe that they can rob us of the power to create wealth:

1. *Pride* lies about the source of all blessing.
2. *Anger* hinders us from working at our best.
3. *Greed* creates financial stagnation.
4. *Lust* robs us of our strength and focus.
5. *Sloth* keeps us from sowing and/or reaping.
6. *Gluttony* causes us to consume all of our seed.
7. *Envy* prevents us from seeing our own blessings.

Resolve now to let the Lord deal with any of these areas that "so easily entangles" you. You'll prosper even as your soul prospers!

Don't doubt in the darkness what God has shown you in the light.

"Immediately Jesus reached out his hand and caught him. 'You of little faith,' he said, 'why did you doubt?'" (Matthew 14:31 NIV).

Three years ago our business shifted from advertising to publishing. I had lots of faith, hope, and enthusiasm. I felt I had heard from God in making such a drastic change. It was to be another "leap of faith" similar to the one I had made ten years earlier when I first went into business.

It appeared to be an easy leap. I felt uniquely prepared, unequivocally called, and totally anointed to take up this "great work" for the Lord!

Then barely after we had gotten started, it seemed as if even heaven had turned against us. We lost a large contract with another publisher. Cashflow slowed to a trickle. Half of our staff took other jobs. I wondered if we could survive another six months. When things seemed darkest, the only thing that kept me going was His word: "I've called you to Mobile to publish, not to be an art director."

Through it all, the Lord *has* provided everything we've needed to do His will. God is so good!

When you're at the center of your power source nothing can touch you!

"He who dwells in the shelter of the Most High will rest in the shadow of the Almighty" (Psalm 91:1 NIV).

Who, or what, is the driving force behind your business? Where do you go for strength when you feel that you can't take another step? How do you respond when all hell seems to break loose against you and your business?

Consider this diagram for a moment:

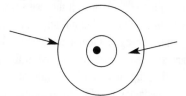

The outer circle represents your sphere of operation, your domain as it were. The inner circle represents your power source. The dot is you. When you live near the center of your power source, hell may be able to touch your domain, but it can't rattle you, deter you from your purpose, or steal your peace. Abide in God!

It's a high calling to serve God in business.

"So I saw that there is nothing better for a man than to enjoy his work, because that is his lot"
(Ecclesiastes. 3:22 NIV, emphasis added).

Many Christian business people have come to believe that they have somehow fallen short of God's purpose for their lives because they're not involved in some sort of "ministry" activity or calling. They think that perhaps God would be more pleased with them if they were a missionary, pastor, or some other kind of full-time minister.

Other people may cause them to think that by being in business they are too closely associated with material things or too preoccupied with making a profit.

While it is definitely possible to get too attached to your business, it is unbiblical to think of any honest work as being second best in God's plan for your life, *if* indeed it *is* God's plan for your life! If God has called you to a business or profession, then do it with all your heart and soul, serving the Lord. As Eric Liddell in *Chariots of Fire* said, "When I run, I feel God's pleasure." If *you* feel His pleasure, you're right where you need to be!

If your house is not in order, it may be the mercy of God to hold back growth.

"Every branch that does bear fruit he trims clean so that it will be even more fruitful" (John 15:2 NIV).

When you're looking for the blessing of the Lord on your business or practice and it seems to be held back, don't assume that God has destined you to a life of poverty. It may be that He needs to prepare you to contain the blessing that He wants to pour out in abundance upon you!

There may be issues in your life that will only get worse if your business grows. Is your business foundation strong enough to bear the weight of a larger structure? Are things at home needing some attention? Is God trying to get your undivided attention over some personal issue?

If God were to double your business within a week, could you handle it? Really? Have you learned how to stay cool when emotions flare in the office? Do you know where to turn for wisdom when you must make an instant decision? Are all your systems in place for tracking and efficiently serving those new customers/clients/patients you so desperately want to add? Like I said, it may be the mercy of God to hold back the blessing until you're ready for it.

Seek first the kingdom of God and all these things will be added to you.

"So do not worry, saying, 'What shall we eat?'...or 'What shall we wear?'...your heavenly Father knows that you need them" (Matthew 6:31-32 NIV).

I've sought for many years to understand the meaning of this verse, especially as it relates to being in business. At first it seems to be saying that by seeking God we will be put on the fast track to receiving all the wonderful material blessings that we could ever want or imagine having.

The scenario goes something like this: "Been seekin' the Lord lately? All right brothers and sisters, get out those wish lists 'cause Santa Claus is comin' to town!"

Now I know you don't really believe like this, but don't we all sometimes wish it worked this way? That's because our hearts are "deceitful above all else." It's because at our human core we are all basically selfish and self-centered.

I have come to believe that this verse speaks of being focused on the Lord in such a deep way that our human needs pale in comparison to knowing Him. Yes, those human needs will be met, but that's not where our heart is.

Y2K means "Yield to the King."

"Watch yourselves closely so that you do not forget the things your eyes have seen or let them slip from your heart as long as you live" (Deuteronomy 4:9 NIV).

When the Y2K warnings started gaining almost fever pitch at the end of 1999, we came up with a t-shirt that said, "Y2K Yield to the King."

At the time many people, including Christians, were very worried about the collapse of our national infrastructure. What we wanted to do with the t-shirt was to point people to the King of Kings—to put their trust in Him and not in our technology.

Y2K came, and 1999 went, the way of all years—resigned to our memories and the history books. No jet crashes were reported; there were no nuclear meltdowns; the electricity kept flowing; and everyone breathed a huge sigh of relief. The sky had not fallen!

So is it back to business as usual? Or, will we remember our vulnerability and our utter dependence on the Living God? For all our sakes, I sincerely hope it's the latter.

Play "Twenty Questions" when evaluating a new business opportunity.

1. Did the idea come from God—will it glorify Him?
2. Is it a *great* idea—can you get excited about it?
3. Does it meet a very real need?
4. Will you be up against a lot of competition?
5. Is this venture compatible with your mission?
6. Have you thoroughly researched the market?
7. Have you completed a business plan?
8. Have you completed a marketing plan?
9. Have you counted the cost—is it worth it?
10. What do trusted advisors think of the idea?
11. Can you test the idea without a lot of capital risk?
12. Does the venture fit your gifts, skills, calling?
13. Does the worst case scenario look profitable?
14. Have others been successful with similar ideas?
15. Does the idea violate any biblical principles?
16. Will your new associates be your kind of people?
17. Will the venture hurt existing relationships?
18. Will it allow you to keep your options open?
19. What does your spouse think of the idea?
20. Do you feel an inner peace about proceeding?

Practice the seven habits of highly-creative business people.

"From now on I will tell you of new things, of hidden things unknown to you. They are created now, and not long ago..." (Isaiah 48:6-7 NIV).

In today's competitive economy, every business needs to be innovative. As one who regularly practices creative problem solving (I have to—I've got lots of problems), I offer the following seven keys to creativity:

1. Tap into God's unlimited creativity through the power of prayer and meditation.

2. Learn and use creative triggers—techniques that help spark creative thinking such as "free association," "right brain" activities, and "what if" questions.

3. Hang around and brainstorm with creative people.

4. Keep a "creativity journal"—jot down ideas as they come to you (it's usually when they're least expected).

5. Get away to one of those favorite places where it's easy for you to relax and be creative.

6. Think outside the box, take risks, break the "rules."

7. Be a kid again: dream big, have fun, and don't worry about what others will think!

Appreciate what you have in common with farmers.

"Still other seed fell on good soil, where it produced a crop—a hundred, sixty or thirty times what was sown" (Matthew 13:8).

Growing a business is a lot like farming:

1) Cultivate the ground—prepare yourself and prepare your field.

2) Save up seed to sow—don't consume all of your seed. Save some so you won't have to borrow.

3) Sow your seed—sow systematically, in rows and fields. It's important to sow in the proper season.

4) Weed and fertilize—weed out the problems and pests that destroy the crop, and fertilize the ground with the lessons of your mistakes.

5) Ask God to send the rain and withhold pestilence.

6) Be patient for the harvest—don't give up and don't harvest your fruit prematurely.

7) Enjoy the harvest—bring in helpers to lighten the work of harvesting.

8) Honor God with the first fruits.

Plan to leave a legacy and inheritance.

"A good man leaves an inheritance for his children's children, but a sinner's wealth is stored up for the righteous" (Proverbs 13:22).

When you retire or die will your business end? Will its impact and influence cease? Or will there be others whom you've trained who will take up the baton? Will you leave an impression on your customers, suppliers, and staff that will endure after you are gone? What is the legacy you will leave behind? What kind of inheritance will you bequeath? Will you leave behind rich memories and life-changing lessons or just the taste of bitter herbs? Will you bequeath a thriving business or estate, or just a pile of long overdue bills?

In your financial planning, don't just plan for *your* retirement. Consider your family and most loyal business associates. But don't just leave it all to them—prepare them to receive it, improve on it, and pass it on to the next generation. Whether it's the business itself or the principles you learned that helped create it—consider the importance of passing it on.

Hang in there, baby– it's not over 'til it's over.

"I have fought the good fight, I have finished the race, I have kept the faith"
(2 Timothy 4:7).

We've had a great response to the first edition of this little book. People have commented on my honesty and vulnerability. This new edition added more of the same.

When I started writing this book, the question came up: "Do we include all of our mistakes or just the lessons learned?" My reply was that the mistakes would temper my words...would add a dimension of reality that might not otherwise be communicated. A lot of business people we know are going through the same things we are. I wanted this book to be relevant to where they are.

If things are going well for you, rejoice! Just don't let complacency catch you off guard.

If times are tough, hang in there. Just when you think it's all over, *things can change—literally—overnight.* If what you have was worth starting, then it's worth fighting for...worth sacrificing for...worth praying for. *Keep the faith!*